CREATING HEAVEN'S
ATMOSPHERE

CREATING HEAVEN'S
ATMOSPHERE

*Experience the tangible reality
of heaven at any time, place and
season of life!*

JOHN BELT

To contact the author:
John Belt | P.O. Box 409 | Ponte Vedra Beach, FL 32004

overflowglobal.com
johnbelt.com

Contents

PREFACE

LORD, I have loved the habitation of Your house,
And the place where Your glory dwells.

Psalms 26:8

Embracing Heaven's Lifestyle

In the beginnings of my walk with God, what I found most invaluable was the ability to create an atmosphere that was so much different than what I was previously accustomed to. The Lord had brought me out of so many bad habits. Without really knowing what I was doing at the time - I knew that my life patterns had to change permanently so I could move into all that God had for my life.

It was a radical shift that I much needed. When I experienced God's power and presence in my life, I knew that the key would be for me to re-create that experience daily. Intellectual knowledge is not what made me free. It was an encounter with the Living God!

Because of this, I embraced a lifestyle of living in God's Presence. As imperfect as it was in my attempts - it eventually became clearer and clearer how this way of life could be reality. Just like anyone else, I had bumps along the way. Yet because

I had learned how to re-create encounters, experiencing God's Presence - it kept me through those times.

God looks for those who will be "faithful" to Him. He wants faithful servants, not perfect people. We get to leave perfection with Him. He is all perfect and all knowing. If anything perfect occurs in our lives, it is because of His Spirit living within us as He works from the inside out. With this book, my goal is to help you learn that it is the will of God for you to walk the way that Jesus walked, that you can create the atmosphere of heaven in your life, and to give you practical ways to make it manifested in your life - every day!

As you read, continually ask the Lord to give you insights, revelation, understanding, and wisdom on how you can apply what's found in this book to your life. A life of wisdom is key to living a life saturated with the glory of heaven.

Why is that? Because anyone can have information and knowledge, but wisdom is the understanding of how to implement what you know. It comes down to surrender. We need to have the motivation to make the right choices in life.

May the Holy Spirit give you ears to hear and eyes to see so that you may experience the fullness of abundant life that Jesus gave His life for. (John *10:10*).

Enjoy His Presence Always!
John Belt

Creating Heaven's Atmosphere

Creating Heaven's Atmosphere

CHAPTER ONE

FLEXIBLE IN THE HANDS OF GOD

And the vessel that he made of clay was marred in the hand of the potter; so he made it again into another vessel, as it seemed good to the potter to make.

Jeremiah 18:4

There are different things that help us to carry the atmosphere of heaven. I don't think there's anything that makes a bigger difference than just to have the glory of God in our lives, upon our lives, where we and other people can encounter the Lord. *God wants people that carry His glory that others may experience Him.*

Carrying heaven's reality comes simply by having a life that is yielded to Jesus. It's not about words. It's not a list of things that you have to do. However, there are some tips - things you can do.

Let the Lord lead you and guide you in your devotion and your times with Him. He wants your relationship to be living and alive rather than mechanical. There is no one certain way to do things. If we get caught up in the

Spiritual disciplines like prayer and Bible study are vital, but they should flow from a heart of love in relationship rather than a checklist.

mechanics of discipline and devotion, we can lose the joy of the experience that is central to our life with God.

I. Yielding to the Spirit
If we get mechanical with spiritual disciplines, we can also become hard on ourselves. You don't ever want to be hard on yourself. *Jesus is not a taskmaster.* He is your Lord, friend and wants to help. That why He sent the Holy Spirit! People who are hard on themselves are most typically hard on others.

When it comes to devotional life with God I set my schedule

and have general plan, but I don't hit it "the same" every time. There are some people who are perfect with their schedules. If that's you, God continue to bless you in that way! It's just not me. I don't hit it every time. I try to make plans happen. Scripture says that a wise man makes plans. We do want to plan some things. God plans things.

If you don't plan at all, you're planning to fail. It's good to have some plans. At the same time, you can't let those plans become a box because a box is very constricting, confining and consequently suffocating! We want to follow the leading of the Holy Spirit. The sons of God are led by the Spirit of God and we want to be led by the Spirit on all occasions. We can have the best of both worlds.

We need a merger between our plans and the leading of the Spirit. The Holy Spirit can lead you to have a plan. There are practical things that help you stay on track.

Do the things that will help power the dreams God has put in your heart. We want to be practical and led by the Spirit. We need to be flexible to also throw away a plan to follow the Spirit. But it's always good to have a plan - an anointed plan is wonderful!

If you're not planning at all you're planning to fail.

II. Heart Felt Worship
Think about orchestrations - a musical score. How beautiful it can be. There are so many ways we can express worship and music - not just one way. I love orchestrations. It's planned.

It's very detailed. God has a lot of detail. In the Old Testament, God had a lot of plans for the tabernacle. He had big plans for the temple.

He is the God of plans. The detail was absolutely excruciating and required a lot of people to accomplish it. God is also very spontaneous – in the moment. He's God of the heart. He wants us to express ourselves in worship to Him from the heart. We can learn everything up in our heads and still never connect with God in our hearts. Yet it doesn't have to be that way. The mind is powerful as God's given it to us. It just needs given over to the Holy Spirit.

We want a library in our minds that serves the Holy Spirit.

It is the best of both worlds. Sowing the seeds of God's Word in our hearts, envisioning the strategic plans that He has for us - these things can be viewed from many angles. There is not just one view or angle to see things from. God is multi-dimensional. He wants to broaden our view and see the fullness of manifestation of His Kingdom on earth as it is in heaven.

One of my sons was learning the books of the Bible - to know all 66 books and to say them in order, and he was doing a great job. But knowing all 66 books in the Bible and having them all in order is not necessarily going to connect you with God from the heart. Even though it's great to know and we want to encourage that - ultimately, your library only serves the Spirit.

We want a library in our minds that serves God's desires as we follow Him from the heart. We need to fill ourselves with all the good things of God. We need to meditate on the things of heaven, things above. We want to be yielded to the Holy Spirit in all things. You can have one way to do something that just turns into a very limited box. It's good to be flexible.

Flexibility is essential not only in our relationship with God but also in our relationships with others.

In church circles it is very common for people to have a "certain way" to do things - it typically comes with that particular church culture. It is not inherently wrong either. However, it does cross a line when we begin to say it is the ONLY way to do something. The gospels were written from four different angles - but all have the same message. Jesus didn't heal a person the same way twice. In that same way, He has a customized plan for each of us as we follow Him.

If I'm to say, this is how it worked for me to get to this point in my life - so this is how it is going to look for you too. That woudn't be true. Everyone has a peculiar path with the Lord. Where the similarities lie would be in seeking God with the whole heart, loving God with a full devotion. As I give you this for advise - it will NEVER fail! It is the path of your life, God specific directions to you, that will be unique.

III. A Divine Parallel of Flexibility
In a marriage, you must be flexible. When you have two people, someone's got to bend. Someone's got to give. Some-

thing's got to give here in order to make this work, because in marriage, you have two different planets coming together as one.

You must be flexible, and you have two worlds coming together. In marriage, people need to understand that before they get married. They don't know what they're getting into. Even if you can have so much in common, it's a different dynamic. The devil hates marriage because it has to do with covenant. It's a picture of Christ and the Church. He wants to destroy marriages. You must realize that there's going to be the need for compromise - in the context of personal preferences. There are going to be things where you work it out. You can't be hardline, legalistic - but you must learn how to love.

Jesus said, in my paraphrase, "You know, you guys need to forgive each other 70 times seven a day." Have you ever given anybody 70 times in one day, just in a day? I mean, I think two times is getting to the hilt. After two times in a day, I'm like, okay, something's not right here. You know, I haven't even hit 10 yet. Jesus says, "This is love - where you literally die to self."

It's the husband's place to lay it down, even more so, because Christ laid His life down for the Church - which is the bride. It's a perfect picture. The point is that we need flexibility. It's an extremely good attribute to have. Be flexible with God because we're in a marriage with Him too! He expects flexibility. He's bent over backwards for us. He's shown us the greatest love. We need to respond to that love by being flexible.

Key Points

- Embrace a life yeilded to the Holy Spirit, as believers in Jesus Christ we are dependent upon Him as He is our Helper.

- As you vocalize your worship to God, don't focus on the formality but the intimacy that you are having with God as your Father. He is looking for those who will worship Him in spirit and in truth - from the heart.

- Forgiveness is not an option, but a commandment that is to be obeyed. This is why we are dependent upon the Holy Spirit to pour God's love in our hearts. It is not of ourselves as much as Him working through us to love others. This again requires dependency upon Him.

- It is always good to have a plan, but learn to be a Spirit-led with flexibility in those plans.

- God has called us to be a people of revelation, not just information. Keep your mind yielded to the Holy Spirit in all things.

Practical Steps

1. *Surrender your heart to God* - laying all thoughts before Him. Find the place of tuning to His heart in worship. God speaks to us as we make room for Him

2. *Begin to schedule* what you beleive God is asking you to do. What are your gifts? What is your contribution to further God's Kingdom? Plan around these things.

3. As you follow your plan *give yourself some flexibility* to be led by the Spirit. Don't be stiff and rigid but allow God to breathe on the specific things He would have you to do. Sometime He will say, "Focus on this particular thing."

4. Take some time to express yourself to God in a new and different way. *Write your own simple song of worship and sing it!*

5. When Jesus was on the cross He said, "Forgive them Father **for they don't know what they are doing.**" Understanding this verse can release grace in your heart to be more forgiving.

CHAPTER TWO

CRUCIFIED LIFE

I am crucified with Christ.
Nevertheless, I live not me, but Christ in me
and the life that I live now.
I live by faith in the Son of God
who loved me and gave himself for me.

Galatians 2:20

Salvation is not this kind of thing where we just want our ticket to heaven. Jesus wants disciples. He wants people who will follow Him, no matter what the cost, no matter what the price. He said, "When you lose your life for My sake, you will find it." He communicated this very clearly - there's no mistake about it. Paul said, "I die daily." This wasn't just a one-time gig. It's a daily choice where you reckon yourself dead, not only to sin, but to self.

Here's our motivation - His love. While we were yet sinners, Christ died for us.

I. The Cost of Righteous Living

Romans 5:7 says, "Someone would die for a good man, but scarcely for a righteous man would someone die." And why is that? Because the righteous man is doing what's right in the eyes of God - telling the world that its ways are bad. People get mad at people who are trying to follow the Lord.

Discipleship requires a daily choice to die to self.

The world cannot hate you, but it hates Me because I testify of it that its works are evil. **John 7:7**

Have you ever had opposition when you're just following Jesus? Many people in this world just don't like it. They don't like to be challenged, offended, and simply love a sinful life-style. Sin means to do something wrong, evil and in rebellion against God's will. The world is in the sway of the evil one. (I John 5:19) People need confronted with the truth that they may get on the right path - Godward.

There is a beautiful side to correction. The Book of Proverbs teaches us that a "wise-man" loves correction, but "a fool" rejects it. The modern day culture of this world being inspired by hell itself is teaching that "you can't offend me". This opens the door for people to be corrected for anything wrong - because it is "offensive" to correct them. If you can't be corrected, the path is downward. This opens the door to all kinds of evil, sin and iniquity. To be corrected, for those who love God, is a blessing because it helps us to stay on course - His course! His path shines brighter and brighter as we continue heavenward.

What does this have to do with "creating heaven's atmosphere?" Everything! You cannot live in contradiction to God's standards and expect to have His blessing and favor. It is necessary for us to go "His direction."

The world may not like the direction you're going. Even those in your family - your distant relatives, the in-laws and the outlaws may not like you. Have you ever had that happen? You're just obeying God, and they're just mad. Scarcely for a righteous man will someone die.

That's what happens when you follow God without compromise. For a good man, a people-pleaser, someone would dare to die. People like a good person. He does everything right "according to what is nice". The good man does the things "I like". I might die for this guy, he is always doing what I like, saying what I like to hear. But a righteous person gets in your way and can be offensive - because he is speaking the truth.

Jesus was the perfect righteous man - God in the flesh. He was killed for telling the truth. He spoke the truth, not for Himself, but to help others see the Light. While we were yet "sinners" Christ died for us. There was nothing that we were doing that we should "deserve" what Jesus gave to us. We were all in rebellion against God. In our worst place, Jesus died for us. At our lowest reprobate state, in this state of ugliness, Jesus died for us. Who is willing to admit that their way of living, attitudes, and thoughts are total refuse to God? Sinners by nature are those who are born into sin. Sinners by lifestyle are those who live a life of sinful choices. God's grace is available to anyone who will recognize and repent from a lifestyle of sin, as well, realizing they are born into it. It is necessary to realize man's problematic spiritual condition. Jesus died for every person in the world, demonstrating His love for us through His cross.

II. Reckoning Ourselves Dead to Sin

Paul says, "I am crucified with Christ. Nevertheless, I live, not me but Christ in me." (Gal. 2:20) Paul declared he was crucified with Christ. When Jesus died, we died. As well, when Jesus rose, we rose in newness of life. When He rose, we rose in the power of His resurrection. It's not about our works. It's not that it's about us being hard on ourselves. That's not how we die. It is by faith in the work of Jesus on the cross. We simply believe and say, "When He died, so did I."

For if we have been united together in the likeness of His death, certainly we also shall be in the likeness of His resurrection, knowing this, that our old man was crucified with Him, that the body of sin might be done away with, that we should no longer be slaves of sin. **Romans 6:5-6**

When He died, it was the most selfless act - the sins of the world were put upon Him. He took our sins on the cross so that we could reckon ourselves dead to sin, and alive to God. Jesus made the way. It's my faith in His work. We say, "Jesus, I see that when you died on the cross, so did I." When you believe that, it is when it becomes living and active in your life. You receive His finished work for you. How many of you want to live that life?

God looks for faithfulness, not perfection.

III. Jesus: The Perfect Example

Jesus paid the price as an example to us. As we desire to see heaven on earth in our lives, we can expect nothing less. God asks us to do things that will cost us. We are living sacrifices. When Jesus was about to go to the cross, Peter told Him that he would die for Him. He was not ready.

Jesus knew his heart had not gone through the process needed for this task - telling Him that he would deny Him three times. Peter was restored, preached on Pentecost, and learned how to be a "living sacrifice" - later in life, he died a martyr's death. We all are called to be living sacrifices. Through seeking the Lord, pursuing Him, living by His voice, running the race - we see Heaven manifested on earth.

The greatest glory came on the heels of the Jesus' sacrifice when He was raised from the dead! The seed of His life gave birth to endless explosions of life from the day of Pentecost forward.

When we take up our cross to follow Jesus it is a daily decision through faith - knowing that when "He died, we died". In our pursuit to follow the Lord our relationship with Him is the priority.

God wants us to offer ourselves as "living sacrifices", hearing His voice and empowered by His Spirit. Anyone can do a good deed but without God it is simply humanism. God calls us to a life of obedience and supernatural works that follows the promptings and power of His Spirit - as we give all glory to Him.

Key Points

- When we take up our cross to follow Jesus it is a daily decision based on the truth that when "He died, we died".
- In our pursuit to follow the Lord our relationship with Him is the priority.
- God wants us to offer ourselves as "living sacrifices", hearing His voice and empowered by His Spirit.
- Anyone can do a good deed but without God it is simply humanism. God calls us to a life of obedience and supernatural works that follows the promptings and power of His Spirit - and give all glory to Him.

Practical Steps

1. *Ask the Lord to give you a revelation* of His love for you - then allowing that to inspire your to follow Him at all costs.
2. When thoughts come that are contrary to God's will quote Galatians 2:20 - *speaking it aloud!*
3. *Ask God to fill you "with grace" to yeild yourself to Him.* Spiritual strength comes from God - realize that He will empower you to do what He has called you to!
4. Set your heart in a position of surrender to God, learning to be flexible.
5. Embrace spiritual disciplines (prayer, study, & worship) to enhance your relationship with God.
6. Make the things of heaven your meditation (promises, truth, Jesus, and spiritual gifts).
7. Walking in love sometimes means we need to be flexible. Our love for God is evidenced in how we love one another.

CHAPTER THREE

INTERACTION WITH THE SPIRIT

I beseech you therefore, brethren,
by the mercies of God, that you present
your bodies a living sacrifice, holy, acceptable
to God, which is your reasonable service.

Romans 12:1

Have you ever struggled to live for God? To be a living sacrifice? Even to just do the things that please Him? Typically, the issue lies in the focus and "the means" of how that is to happen. It is through tending to our relationship with God, *our communion with the Spirit,* and focus on the Lord that we are transformed and able to live after His desires. It's all about the relationship.

I. Inside Out

As the Spirit lives inside of us, *He puts to death the deeds of the flesh* as we walk in His truth. This works through our communion with the Holy Spirit – our interaction with Him. The Spirit is not to be ignored, as *Jesus told us that He would be our Helper.* (John 16:7)

We want to learn how to create an atmosphere of God's Presence – to carry His glory no matter where we are. We want the atmosphere of heaven to be in us through the Person of the Holy Spirit. Our lives should be saturated with the Spirit's Presence.

> *The Holy Spirit is the Helper Jesus gave to us to help us here on Earth.*

"But we have this treasure in earthen vessels, that the excellence of the power may be of God and not of us."
2 Corinthians 4:7

As this happens, the Spirit Himself manifests joy, peace, power, and the love of God. These attributes of God are the fruit of the Spirit - and cannot be produced without His Presence. The love of God flows freely through us as we live yielded to the Spirit. He is the source of love. He is the source of life. We are created to be temples of the Holy Spirit.

II. Inhabited & Anointed

God wants to inhabit you, just like His glory filled the temple in the days of Moses. He wants to come by His Spirit to manifest His Presence beyond what you can imagine. Jesus was anointed with the Spirit without measure. He's called us to be anointed in the same way.

The purpose of the Son of God manifest was to destroy the works of the devil – to obliterate the works of the devil. We are called to do the same thing. You're called to carry that same anointing that sets people free. (1 John 3:8)

One of the ways we can begin to carry God's Presence is by simply spending time with Him. This is part of our surrender. Learning to practice the Presence of God is essential for our lives. We want to absorb all that God is and has for us. Just as whatever you put inside your body will be what you feel like. Eat something healthy, and you will feel healthy. Eat unhealthy things, and you will be unhealthy. You are what you eat. How much more should we hunger and thirst for God!

III. Finding Consistency

God has made us like sponges. We absorb what we hang around. If you've ever put water on a sponge, at the beginning, the sponge is dry and resistant. Have you noticed that initially when you put the sponge under the water, it will bounce off? But after a while, after just a little bit of time, it begins to absorb the water. Once it is broken in, it's amaz-

ing how much water it can hold! We are much like sponges.
Soaking in the Presence of God is like this. You have to give

God loves it a little time. Be consistent. Learn how to
when we sit just hang out with God. He loves that! And so
at His feet. should we.

*LORD, I have loved the habitation of Your house, And the place
where Your glory dwells.* **Psalms 26:8**

How do you do this? I like to just turn on some worship,
instrumentals – things that have anointing. Just hang out, lie
on the couch, whatever you want, on your bed, wherever, and
you just spend time receiving from the Lord. Receiving from
God is very important.

Religion makes it all about your works – rather than tending
to your relationship with God. But the Lord loves it when we
will sit at His feet like Mary did – receiving His words, enjoy-
ing His Presence. (Luke 10:38-42)

You don't have an agenda. You're not coming to pray a bunch
of prayers, to remind God of everything He needs to do for
you. You're just there as a child in a sense, just receiving from
the Father. We need that childlike faith. God loves it when we
have simple faith. Just say to the Lord, "I just receive everything you have for me."

Key Points

- The Holy Spirit changes us from the "inside out". This is the difference between having religion vs. having relationship.
- Spending time with God is the key to being able to carry His Presence - to transform atmospheres.
- God has a habitation and He has made us to be habitations, dwelling places, for His glory and Presence.
- With religion the focus is on our works, with the Spirit-filled life the focus is on being dependent on the work of Christ and how He is working on the inside of us to do His good pleasure.

Practical Steps

1. Begin to create your history with God through worship alone with Him. *Make it a quality time of quiet simplicity in His Presence.*
2. How have you experienced God's presence filling you during times of worship or prayer?
3. What does it mean to you to carry the same anointing as Jesus to set others free?
4. Take a few minutes to prioritize spending time with God - *open up Romans 8 marking keywords and making notes with your thoughts on the passages.*
5. *Use soaking music to create and atmosphere to connect with God.*

CHAPTER FOUR

KNOWING THE FATHER

When you pray, go into your room.
And when you have shut the door, pray to your Father,
who is in the secret place. And your Father
who sees in secret will reward you openly.

Matthew 6:6

Hear what Jesus is saying here. At this time, the idea of God being Father was new. People understood God. They knew "God Almighty", but Jesus was saying, "your Father". This was a new revelation. This was something that the Pharisees and the religious leaders could not understand. They were offended when Jesus talked about the Father as He was making Himself equal with God. He made it clear that He was part of the family, the Son of the Father's house. They understood the power of inheritance and understood the position He was claiming.

I. Revelation of the Father

In the same way, Jesus wants us to get a revelation of the Father.

"Your Father, Who sees in secret, will reward you openly." **Matt. 6:6**

By abiding in the secret place, we reflect His love and power, creating an environment where His kingdom is tangible.

As you go into the secret place,
hang out with your Father in heaven as a son or daughter, He's going to reward you openly. He doesn't say, "Go in there and pray all your prayers and give a litany of things to do." He just wants you to go into that place to hang out with Him. David understood this. He had revelation, as we read Psalm 91. He had New Testament understandings in the Old Testament.

"He who dwells in the secret place of the Most High shall abide under the shadow of the Almighty." **Psalm 91**

II. Benefits of Dwelling in the Secret Place

There are so many blessings that come just because of dwelling in the secret place. Just because you dwell with Him, doing this one thing, there's so much blessing that comes to you. Jesus says, the Father is going to reward you openly as you spend time in the secret place.

We want people who know the secret place. People who love to hang out with God. As we learn to develop communities that dwell in God's Presence like this, when everybody comes together, the manifested glory of God will be so much stronger.

This is something that you will have to be willing to train yourself into. Sin comes naturally, righteousness doesn't. You have to realize that your spirit is much more real than your flesh. You have to bring selfish desires under the power of the Spirit and yield to God. Especially in the initial stages of your spiritual walk, you have a battle that goes on inside of you between your old desires and the new person that you are in Christ - the spirit man.

You have to choose to feed your spirit, rather than satisfy the lusts of your flesh. If you never get beyond your selfish preferences, you will have a most miserable Christian life. No Presence of God, no reality of Him being with you - because by continually making the wrong choices you stay immature. Jesus calls us to the secret place - your very best choice.

We find our identity in Him alone.

III. Sons and Daughters of the Secret Place

Don't live like an orphan, outside of His courts, outside of the secret place. Learn that your Father, Who is in that secret place, is waiting for you. When you spend time with your Father, He's going to reward you openly in so many different ways. Dwell in Him. Abide in the Vine, Jesus.

Everyone finds their identity in something. People look for it in positions, possessions, power and other things. It really isn't "what you know" but "WHO you know." As you spend time with God you are developing a history before Him. You are developing a "trust". No one trusts just anybody. God trusts us to the level that we will get to know Him. Spending time with God is valuable in every way. Most want to do something for God without spending any time with God. Unless God is building something it is no eternal value. That's why Jesus told us to "abide" in Him.

"Do not be deceived, God is not mocked; for whatever a man sows, that he will also reap. 8 For he who sows to his flesh will of the flesh reap corruption, but he who sows to the Spirit will of the Spirit reap everlasting life." **Galatians 6:7-8**

In the measure that we sow, is the measure that we will reap. What we sow is what will grow. When we sow to the Spirit we will reap life. If we sow to the flesh we will reap corruption - that which won't last. We should continually be spending our time devoted to what is of eternal value. This is where we find our identity in Him. In Christ we are complete. Paul counted all things loss just to know Jesus in fullness - to be identified with Him in the fellowship of His sufferings as he walked a completely different path than the world. (Phil. 3:10) This is where we find our true identity.

Key Points

- The Father rewards us as He finds us in the secret place of His Presence.
- We have always been given "the choice"! We have the ability to choose to dwell in His Presence - responding to His invitation.
- Our identity is not found in titles, positions, platforms and power - but in knowing Him. We are sons and daughters of God - this is our true identity.

Practical Steps

1. As you spend time in the Secret Place with God in your personal devotional times *EXPECT God to reward you openly - He loves to see faith!*
2. Jesus told Phillip, "When you've seen me, you've seen the Father." (John 14:9) *Meditate on this with a fresh perspective of God as your Father.*
3. *Gather together with other worshippers that are hungry for more of God* and experience greater manifestation of His glory in worship!

CHAPTER FIVE

A LIFE OF MEDITATION

Let the words of my mouth
and the meditation of my heart
Be acceptable in Your sight,
O LORD, my strength and my Redeemer.

Psalms 19:14

We've talked about dwelling in the Father, dwelling in the secret place, and just learning to love communion with God. There's no place you would rather be than in the Presence of God. Better is one day in His courts than a thousand elsewhere. That's the foundation. The next thing is your meditation, your thought life.

"Finally, brethren, whatever things are true, whatever things are noble, whatever things are just, whatever things are pure, whatever things are lovely, whatsoever things are of good report, if there is any virtue or anything praiseworthy, meditate on these things. The things which you learned and received and heard and saw in me, these do, and the God of peace will be with you." **Philippians 4:8-9**

I. The Power of Renewing Your Mind

This was one of my favorite verses when I first got saved because I needed a renewed mind, a new way of thinking and wasn't raised in church. I knew my mind needed some major renovation. This passage helped me a lot. This revealed to me what I needed to focus on and think about. Notice that all of this is really very positive and good. I had a big amount of negativity growing up. In my life, things that happened to me weren't really from my family. It was just the accumulation of negative experiences. I had to change my mindset, change my focus, and this passage really helped me.

God loves to break natural laws with His truth.

It's thinking about the things that are true according to God's Word rather than the lies. What does God say? That settles it. We do have facts, natural laws. God loves to break natural laws with His truth. His truth breaks into our natural world. Facts bow to His truth. When Jesus healed the blind man, it changed the fact that he was blind into the fact that he could see. Heaven's truth that there are no blind people in heaven was made manifest in the blind man so he would be blind no more. When you get revelation of the truth, you have the grace and ability to see it manifest in your life.

The practice of meditation on God's Word roots us in His reality.

You may not feel healed. But the Word of God says, "By His stripes, you are healed." That truth changes your current circumstances, as you believe it, and as you receive it, and as you meditate on it. Whatever things are true - you make that your meditation. You make the Word of God your meditation.

II. Holiness Through the Holy Spirit

As we continue to look at this verse, it says, "Whatever things are noble, just, pure." God deals with our spiritual condition - our lifestyle. This is a different issue. When the stuff that comes through the TV set is unclean, most of it's not pure. You don't want to focus on sin and iniquity. As you sow thoughts in your heart, you will reap those same things. You don't want to focus on sin. You want to focus on that which is pure, pleasing to the Lord, that which is holy. Without holiness, no one will see God. Also, if you're not free from it, how are you going to help someone who's in it? You won't be able to help them. If you don't have purity in your heart, you're not going to be able to help someone who is struggling. We have to have a pure heart.

"Who shall ascend to the hill of the Lord, but he who has clean hands and a pure heart - who has not lifted up his soul to an idol."
Psalm 24:3

There are many idols in the Old Testament. There are many idols today, even American idols. We've sugar-coated idols today. In our modern day, they're just shrouded in a different form where we don't recognize them as easily. It's not about how you look on the outside. It's not the externals. It's not changing all that stuff of how you look. It's not how you dress. Will He change your outward behavior and appearance? When needed. Yes. But that is not man's job, it comes by revelation as we yield to the Spirit.

The Holy Spirit is the Helper because we need help!

Holiness comes from the Holy Spirit working on the inside of our hearts. There is no holiness apart from the Holy Spirit. If you ignore the Holy Spirit, you have a fake version of holiness - a counterfeit. It's not the real deal. The Holy Spirit is the only one who can make us holy. That's why His first name is "Holy". It makes sense doesn't it? Are you really going to be holy without the Holy Spirit dwelling inside of you? Get my point? He's the Person who transforms us. He is the Helper that Jesus sent to us for empowerment both internally and for others. We need the Holy Spirit because we need help!

III. Tuning Into God's Frequency
Philippians 4 goes on to mention meditating on the good report. We don't want to think about all the bad reports. The news seems like 99.9% bad reports. I like to stay in tune with

the needed news, but most of it is a soap-opera and entertainment. It's a business, so they have to have news even if it stinks. Most of it you don't even need to know about. What news does God have for you each day? Think about that. Does His news matter to you?

In order to get God's news, you have to tune into His frequency. You have to spend time with Him. Are you doing that? God wants His Words to be your meditation day and night. We want to think on the good reports. What are the good reports of what God is doing? Get the inside info by spending time with God - reading His Word. He longs to reveal His secrets. Most everything that God does won't be showing up in the media. When someone is healed, raised from the dead - in most cases, it's not going to get in the mainstream media.

Paul says, If there's any virtue, if there's anything praiseworthy, meditate on these things - the things which you learned and received and heard and saw in me, these do, and the God of peace will be with you. Paul is living it. He's also saying you can live this.

"Blessed is the man who meditates in the law of the Lord day and night. He shall be like a tree planted by the rivers of living water, bearing fruit in season. His leaf does not wither, and whatever he does shall prosper." **Psalm 1:1-3**

You want that to be you? And the choir said, "AMEN!"

"If then you were raised with Christ, seek those things which are above where Christ is, sitting at the right hand of God. Set your mind on things above, not on things of the earth, for you died."
Colossians 3:1-3

As we change what we meditate upon it creates healthy strongholds around the mind. In essence, we are pulling down the old thinking, bad strongholds, and replacing them with good ones! Habits are habits. You choose your habits. It is not that hard. I've heard it said that it takes 30 days of consistency to establish a new pattern or habit. Once you have established it, it comes so much easier.

What God calls us to He also gives us the grace to do. He doesn't put on us unrealistic expectations - but things that challenge us to depend on Him. Without Him, we would be in trouble because we couldn't do it. Thankfully, we can do all things through Christ who strengthens us! (Phil. 4:13)

Key Points

- Our habits and thinking patterns are transformed as we renew our minds in God's Word. To "renew" is not a one time event - but something that involved consistency. Create a pattern of renewal in your life.
- Holiness is not about externals, but about the Holy Spirit transforming us from the inside out. God is Holy - we want to be like Him. But this only happen by the indwelling of the Holy Spirit. Otherwise it becomes our works rather than His work that purifies the heart.
- Meditation of God's Word as we seek "those things above" helps us tune to His frequency - becoming more sensitive to the Spriit rather than the things of this world.

Practical Steps

1. Meditate on/read Colossians Chapter 3. Read it over and over again until it becomes a part of you.
2. Embrace holiness by welcoming the Holy Spirit continually - saying, "Come Holy Spriit!"
3. Begin to recognize bad habit or thinking patterns. Find scriptures that bring new formed habits into your life. Focus on things above, not things of the earth.
4. Replace old habits with new good habit that glorifies God and puts Him first in your life.
5. Find others who have the same desires to pursue God - leaving the old relationships behind if they heading a different direction.

CHAPTER SIX

THE WORDS
OF YOUR MOUTH

*Death and life are in
the power of the tongue,
And those who love it will eat its fruit.*

Proverbs 18:21

We've looked at spending time in the Presence of God through out meditation - which is a must. It is a practice we need in our lives. It's the starting point. Our meditation also has the power to shift the atmosphere we carry. We want heaven's atmosphere in our lives.

I. The Innate Power of the Tongue

"We all stumble in many things."
James 3:2

We all stumble. This is not about perfectionism. If anyone does not stumble in word, he is a perfect man. That's an amazing statement.

> *Our meditation shapes the atmosphere we carry, but our words give it voice.*

"If anyone doesn't stumble in word he is a perfect man, able also to bridle the whole body. Indeed, we put bits in horses' mouths, that they may obey us, and we turn their whole body. Look also at ships. Although they are so large and are driven by fierce winds, they are turned by a very small rudder, wherever the pilot desires. Even so, the tongue is a little member, but it boasts great things."
James 3:2-5

The tongue is one of the smallest pieces of your body, but it has an incredible impact. See how great a forest a little fire kindles - seen those fires in California? Someone just drops a cigarette and causes hundreds of thousands of acres to burn up just by one little cigarette, not even a flame that causes all that to burn up.

The tongue is a fire - a world of iniquity. Iniquity is like generational sin. The idea is that sin just passes on and passes on - until Jesus breaks it off our lives. People sin, then you have generational sin. It spreads like wildfire. It spreads and keeps spreading from generation to generation.

II. Speaking with Inspiration from Heaven

Every word Jesus spoke was inspired by the world of His glory - heaven itself being manifested on earth. Every word He spoke. He said, "Heaven and earth shall pass away, but My words will never pass away." They were eternal words. Eternal life was coming out of His mouth. That's what we want for our lives.

"The tongue is also set among our members, that it defiles the whole body and sets on fire the course of nature. And it is set on fire by hell itself." **James 3:6**

That doesn't sound very promising. For us, it doesn't sound very helpful. However there is good news! If you have the Holy Spirit, He can tame your tongue. The Holy Spirit can reign in your speech. You just have to yield to the Holy Spirit. Life and death are in the power of the tongue.

With my family, but not limited to, I'm keenly aware of how important my words are that I speak, not only to my wife, but my kids. I want them to grow up with faith, confidence and be able to do things I was never able to do growing up. My ceiling is their floor. With each generation, things shouldn't get harder - but easier. At least this should be our desire as parents and leaders. There will always be challenges, work and all the things that go with life - but as parents we can make a significant difference and help them accelerate at another level above what we did. In this, what we speak does make a difference as we want our speech and actions to be in unison - sending a clear and encouraging message.

Even if some in your family is giving you a difficult time, your words and actions can shift their behavior. Sometimes it just takes some extra time and effort. Prayer for sure! Seek the Lord to give you wisdom in what to do and say to reverse a course of behavior. Don't relegate it only to prayer - find creative God-inspired ways that thwart the devil's plans. A little love and kindness and reduce the amount of prayer needed. Don't underestimate the arsenal that God has given at your disposal! Don't fall for the lie that you are the only one who deals with difficult things.

Some situations are more difficult than others. But also realize that God gives you power to change these things. Sometimes we think it takes a major miracle when in essence it is can be something very small in our actions and words that causes others to move a different direction. At times it can be a change in us that is needed. At times I've heard many people say, "It's spiritual warfare!" Well maybe. Maybe you just need to learn to love, be kind and do something practical to be a blessing. Our natural actions are just as spiritual as our prayers. Check your own heart and intimacy with God. Let Him speak to you personally.

We can speak life. We can be vessels that are yielded to God. We can speak life over individuals and speak life over ourselves. Speak promises of God's Word. Speak the blessings of God over your life. Don't speak curses. Can you think of anything that you've spoken over yourself in the last week? Things you should not have said? That is creating an atmosphere. Your tongue is powerful.

III. Words Aligned with God's Truth

The tongue is a powerful tool to create atmosphere. By the words that you speak, you create an atmosphere! Some words are neutral. But there is much that we say that we shouldn't say. There's so much that we need to yield to God. Father, forgive US right? I love the Lord's Prayer because it's not only about you. It doesn't say, "Father, forgive me." It's "Father, forgive US." Forgive us our trespasses, as we forgive those who trespass against us. God puts it in the corporate context.

We are one body - the Body of Christ. When one part suffers, the entire body suffers. We want to bring us all together and say, "Father, forgive us and cleanse us all." In this way, we can walk together in unity and the power of the Spirit. It's very important what we speak and demonstrate the love of God as we keep a heart of thanksgiving. It's so important to live in the Presence of God - dwelling in the Secret Place. In the secret place, let your meditation be on things above. Let your meditation be the Word of God. Let YOUR life be aligned with His Word and His truth.

"For the Word of God is quick and powerful, sharper than any two-edged sword, piercing to the dividing asunder of soul and spirit."
Hebrews 4:12

That's what the Word of God does. It discerns and divides between what's coming from your soul, your mind, will, and emotions, versus the new creation that you are - your spirit man or the inner man.

Key Points

- Our tongue can be powerful in both good and bad ways. It is a powerful built-in influencer that God has given to us - as we are created in His image.
- We must consecrate our words and speech to the LORD so that we are speaking that which creates life, helps our own soul and others.
- The tongue is an atmosphere-changer! The words we speak have the ability to shift atmospheres, create environments, both good and bad.
- As believers we must use our words to help bring God's Kingdom realities on earth - on earth as it is in heaven.

Practical Steps

1. Begin your day *reading God's Word aloud* in your private times.
2. *Declare the promises of God* over your life and family. Ex. "Thank You for Your Kingdom Come and Will being done in our lives today." Expand on this as the Spirit leads.
3. *Pay attention to what you are thinking and saying.* Is is a lie? Or is it God's truth as revealed in His Word. Take captive every thought and make it submit to God's truth.

Creating Heaven's Atmosphere

CHAPTER SEVEN

SPIRIT TO SPIRIT

*"No one knows the thoughts of man
except the spirit that is within him.
And no one knows the thoughts of God
except the Spirit of God."*

I Corinthians 2:8

We have been "born again" of the Holy Spirit. We have been made alive to God. In Christ, we have a new spirit that's awakened to the Spirit of God. This is the new creation that God has made us. It is a new day for every one of us because of this experience and change in our lives. Before I was radically committed to Jesus, I was invited by a friend to a little Baptist church in rural Oklahoma when I was around age 16.

On a typical Sunday morning, I heard the message of salvation with an invitation to be water baptized in the evening. Without hesitation, I responded to that call. When I was baptized that evening, I can remember coming out of the waters of baptism feeling totally transformed! Afterwards, I went to my friend's house, and he was shocked at the way I was acting because I was so different. I was acting different and talking like a totally new person.

I. Born Into God's Kingdom

That day, something wonderful had happened to me that I could not put into words. It is what happens when we come to Christ with nothing but desperation and surrender. I discovered there was something I needed that I didn't even know I needed! There is a freshness and renewing of the Holy Spirit that transforms us. It is like a "jump start" with the quickening of His Presence.

Spiritual rebirth awakens our spirit to commune with God.

It was like I lost all these heavy weights on my back. I felt light as a feather! There was such an exceeding joy that I couldn't stop talking. It was a picture of when you deal with things in your spiritual life how it actually affects you physically. My countenance had changed and I was re-invigorated for life again. It would be like my heart jumped back to the condition or feeling it had when I was an infant - before all the garbage that accumulated over all those years.

This is what happens to people. I don't think many realize just how much stuff is accumulated over the years, decades and time. There can be a mountain of spiritual trash that hasn't been dealt with - causing a great deal of heaviness, sadness, disappointment and heartache. It just builds up over the years. Because of this some don't make it through life too far. It's just too much for people to handle. We weren't created to carry that kind of burden. It takes God to knock it off of us so that we can start fresh again.

That is why you have terms like "re-vival" or "re-newal" or "re-focus" or "re-freshing". The list goes on and on. You get the idea. God is an expert at giving us a "re-start". He knows how He made us and He is the only One Who can fix us! He knows what we need. We need the Helper - the Holy Spirit. He is the only One Who can Help us.

II. The Need for More of God

But after that time of my initial salvation experience, I had no clue of what to do. It wasn't until a few years later that I would recommit my life to Christ - then to experience God in an even greater measure through the Baptism in the Holy Spirit. It was a separate experience altogether! Then I was empowered in a new way to "live" the life God called me to live.

Through this, I learned how to commune with the Holy Spirit through worship and speaking in tongues. Just like Paul says - I pray with my spirit and with the understanding.

"For if I pray in a tongue, my spirit prays, but my understanding is unfruitful. What is the conclusion then? I will pray with the spirit, and I will also pray with the understanding. I will sing with the spirit, and I will also sing with the understanding."
I Corinthians 14:14-16

Thankfully, I had not been raised in church to be indoctrinated against this most wonderful aspect of life in God! What is important to realize is that you can become a zealot or religious about anything. Just because you speak in tongues does not mean you cannot become a religious person.

What I mean by that is you can pray in your unknown language and still be dry as a doornail! The main focus always needs to be our relationship with God as we tend to the garden of our hearts. Your thinking and motives are very important. *It all works together to create a heart that is on God's hotline!* With that being said and our focus on the Lord - all that God gives will cause us to flourish in the courts of His Presence! We just need to keep all things about Him as Jesus is the center.

We have to quiet our souls before God - allowing Him to speak to us.

God wants to fill us with His fullness. He peels back the things of our lives layer by layer - going deeper and deeper. *We have to quiet our souls before God - allowing Him to speak to us.* His words are life to our hearts. When He speaks it carries all the essential spiritual ingredients that we need to experience refreshing, renewing and to be revived in His Presence.

As it is, most everyone wants to have "the formula" to success - no matter what it concerns. For our spiritual lives it is not a formula, but a Person. The relationship, if you will, is the formula that we need. God is the essential *Our spirit* ingredient that is missing from our lives - the *is where* essential ingredient that makes everything *we connect* work. He is the glue that brings forth unity in *with God.* people, families and His Body. He has to be the center of all things for our lives.

III. Spirit to Spirit Communion

God gives us His Holy Spirit. Communion with the Holy Spirit is essential in our walk with God. Jesus makes it clear that we are to depend on the Helper, the Holy Spirit, to lead us into all truth. It is a spirit-to-Spirit life with God. Paul paints this picture in the book of 1 Corinthians. God has a Spirit - the Holy Spirit. Man also has a spirit. Our spirit is where we connect with God. He comes into the deepest part of us.

If you were to take the temple in the Old Testament as a picture, there was the outer court, the inner court, and the Holy of Holies. The spirit of man would be parallel with the Holy of Holies - as the holiest place. God comes to dwell in us to have spirit-to-Spirit interaction - as the ultimate communion happens on the inside of us. Worship happens here. Your soul is like the inner court. Then the outer court is your flesh, your body. If we look at it through the lens of loving God, we are told to love God with all of our heart, soul, and strength. There is a lot of depth here in this passage.

"You shall love the LORD your God with all your heart, with all your soul, and with all your strength." **Deuteronomy 6:5**

The word "heart" would refer to the mind or intellect - loving God with our mind. The word for "soul" here is "nephesh" which means breath or spirit. This calls us to love God with our spirit. This would speak of a life of communion with God - our spirit to His Spirit. This is where our simplicity of worship and prayer is expressed. Then "strength" refers to our "passion". Just as we would be totally sold out and excited about something - God wants that directed toward Him! When we combine these three aspects of our lives, mind, spirit, and passion together, we learn to love God with all that we are.

Loving God is the priority. In our pursuit of loving God with a whole heart we realize that we still need Him just to do this! It is only by His grace that we can be all that He has created us to be. There is a place in our walk where we find loving God is just a pleasure. Although it is a commandment, there is a point where it crosses a threshold where you would never consider anything else. As we create heaven's atmosphere in our lives - it is comprised of some things that maybe we would consider "elementary" - whether it be no compromise to sin, sowing to the Spirit, a life of worship, how we speak and other. (a spiritually-sensitive life)

Some of these things you may have heard before. However, these core foundational truths are the anchors that position us in deep waters to discover the consistency of His glory and Presence for our lives - and the lives of those around us. Coupled with the understanding of devotional living, there are deep wells of glory waiting for "whosoever will" to be tapped into. With these wells of the Spirit, we are able to create consistent realms of reality with His glory and Presence upon our lives. In that, creating an atmosphere of heaven in our lives and for the lives of others.

Key Points

- When we are "born again" our spirit is awakened to God. Here we've entered the Kingdom of God and have been made a part of His family.
- The Baptism in the Holy Spirit is "sometimes" a secondary experience where the heavenly language of our spirit is released to "pray with our spirit" or otherwise named "praying in tongues".
- Quieting our souls before God is very core to our ability to hear God as there is much noise to distract us. We must learn to quiet ourselves in His Presence.
- Communion with the Holy Spirit happens as our spirit "connects" with God's Spirit. This is where the most sacred connection with God is found in our devotional times with Him.

Practical Steps

1. If you have not given your life to God, confess your sins to Him, ask Him to forgive you and cleanse you from all the things you've done wrong. Surrender your life to Him - give Jesus Christ all you are.
2. If you have not received the Baptism in the Holy Spirit, ask the LORD to fill you with His Spirit. Say, "Holy Spirit come fill my heart with Your Preseence!"
3. Get your Bible, pick a verse and meditate on it. Be honest with God and keep asking Him to fill you to overflowing with His Presence.
4. Turn on some worshipful instrumental or soft worship music that helps you relax in God's Presence. Practice this daily and grow in His Presence!

Are you ready to discover God's tangible reality?

Creating Heaven's Atmosphere will help you to understand how to bring the atmosphere of heaven to your life on a consistent basis - and bring others there as well!

If you feel dry and empty all the time. That is not normal Christianity. Jesus paid the highest price that you might live in His Presence. Don't settle for less but access the glory of His Spirit to walk in the fullness of His life!

John Belt is an inspired speaker, writer, worship leader. With messages on the life of breakthrough, intimacy with God and Holy Spirit living John shares with joy and humor truth that helps others connect with the fullness of God's life. His passion is to help others enter into a greater personal and corporate experiences in God's glory and Presence.

John is author of the book "The Secret to Experiencing God's Presence" published by Chosen Books and has produced a broad variety of 30 plus albums, both instrumental and worship, to create an atmosphere of worship and prayer. These have been used around the world for people's personal devotional lives.

The Secret to Experiencing God's Presence Book
John Belt

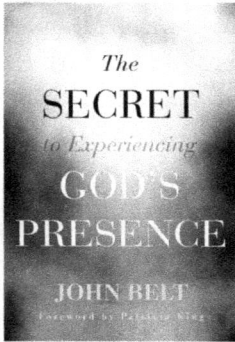

It's easy to feel close to God while worshiping in church, raising our voices and our hearts with other believers as his presence permeates the atmosphere. Unfortunately, for many Christians, this is the only place they experience God's presence. But the Sunday morning experience shouldn't be the exception; it should be the norm.

With wisdom and insights gained from years as a pastor and worship leader, John Belt has helped thousands of believers overcome seasons of spiritual dryness and encounter God's presence every day--and he can help you do the same. Full of inspiring stories and practical tools, this book outlines simple steps to experiencing God personally, reveals potential roadblocks, and gives you the keys to overcoming them. Here is the secret to experiencing God's presence and living victoriously and abundantly every single day.

In the Heavens Album
John Belt

Enjoy this new worship release by John Belt titled "In the Heavens"! This music was created from a prophetic experience some years ago which has now been put into full orchestratin. You will be drawn into the Presence of God as you use this for your worship, devotional, study and exercise times!

Songs Include:

In the Book
In the Heavens
Oh Holy God
The Word of the Lord
You Love Us So Much
Your Anointing
Your Anointing (UFO)

Discover more resources, join us for upcoming events and get equipped for God's purposes and plans for your life!

FIND OUT MORE AT
overflowglobal.com
johnbelt.com

Creating Heaven's Atmosphere

www.ingramcontent.com/pod-product-compliance
Lightning Source LLC
Chambersburg PA
CBHW060038050426
42448CB00012B/3070